ADVENTURES in WILD PLACES

Packed full of Activities and over 250 Stickers

This little wild boar is hiding in this book! Look for him on every main sticker scene.

BAVARIA

THE EVERGLADES

THE RED SEA

THE AMAZON

THE GALÁPAGOS

KRUGER NATIONAL PARK

Can you find the
jellyfish bobbing in
the water?
Can you spot the diver
exploring the underwater
world?

2

WILD WORLD

Wow! This picture shows all of the countries in the world. It shows all the wild places in your book.

RANTHAMBORE

HUANGLONG

MARIANA TRENCH

THE OUTBACK

There's a flag for each place you'll be exploring. Find the matching stickers at the end of your book and stick them in the right places.

3

READY TO GO!

Make an adventure pass to explore wild places!
First write your details, then add your stamp stickers.

MY ADVENTURE PASS

Name

Age

Stick your stamps here.

Draw your face here.

WILD PLACES POSTCARD

Draw what you did today on the postcard. Then write the name of someone to send it to.

Don't forget to create a stamp!

4

Sawu bona

We're going on safari in Kruger National Park, South Africa. Look out for lions, cheetahs, elephants, and rhino with us!

SOUTH AFRICA

This is a 5 rand coin!

Stick what you need in the bag! Don't forget a water bottle, hat and sunglasses!

Did you know that the name rhinoceros means 'nose horn' and is often shortened to rhino? And that a group of rhinoceros is called a 'herd' or a 'crash'?

An exciting way to see the animals is from a hot air balloon. It floats high above the land.

Quick! Point to the cheetah who has climbed on a safari truck!

Have a roarsome time adding all kinds of wild animals to Kruger.

6

Giraffe babies are taller than grown-ups even when they're first born! Give this giraffe mum some children.

People come to **KRUGER NATIONAL PARK** in South Africa to see amazing wild animals. They travel in trucks and watch lions play, cheetahs climb and rhinos charge right in front of them.

Zzzzzzz

Look closely. Can you see a zebra hiding in the long grass?

How many zebra can you count?

CHARGING WILDEBEEST

Can you catch the wildebeest and fill their horns in with your brightest crayons?

Can you spot the lion? Make him bright and bold.

EGYPT

Dive into the Red Sea, Egypt. Meet all sorts of amazing creatures. Let's swim with parrotfish, sea turtles and manta rays!

Marhaba

The largest and most famous pyramid is called The Great Pyramid. It was made for the Pharaoh Khuf and took 20 years to build.

It's time to pack! Can you stick everything into the suitcase? Don't forget your goggles, towel and flip flops.

This is an Egyptian pound coin.

You can call me humuhumu for short.
Stick lots of different creatures into the sea for the divers and snorkelers to see.
Can you spot a snapping shrimp? They have a big claw that makes a very loud SNAP!
The coral in a reef is alive. If it's bright, it's happy, but when it's sick it turns white. Add some happy pink coral to cover these white patches.

This blue and yellow fish with a crazy name is on a trip from Hawaii! Pop on another and say hello humuhumunukunukuapua'a (this is how to say it: who moo who moo noo koo noo koo ah pooah ah).

THE RED SEA coral reef is like an underwater city. Creatures dive, dart around and daydream in the nice warm water.

Divers wear special tanks full of air so they can breathe under the water.

DANCING DOLPHINS

The dolphins are having fun splashing around. Tickle their tummies with your crayons.

Can you find the dolphin flipping upside down?

How many starfish can you spot? Paint them orange.

Olá

BRAZIL

We're exploring the Amazon rainforest in Brazil. You can help us to spot cheeky capybaras, brilliant parrots and screeching howler monkeys! And watch out for the pink dolphins.

This is a Brazilian REAL.

Stick your stickers in the boat and sail down the river.

The Amazon River comes from seven different countries: Guyana, Ecuador, Venezuela, Bolivia, Brazil, Colombia and Peru.

Find your Amazon stickers and fill the rainforest with lots of tropical creatures.

The capybara is the largest rodent in the world. They like to live together in big groups. Give this one a couple of friends.

Hi! I'm a tapir.

...fcutter ants can ...y 50 times their ...n body weight. ...'s a bit like you ...ng a car above your head.

Scientists think half of all life on earth is here in **THE AMAZON** Rainforest! Creatures live everywhere, from the very bottom of the river to the tops of the trees.

Hoooooooowl!

The call of a howler monkey can be heard for 3 to 4 miles (around 6 km), even through the thick tropical rainforest.

Pink Amazon River dolphins feast on over 50 types of fish that they find on the river bottom, and the occasional turtle.

Snap! Snap!

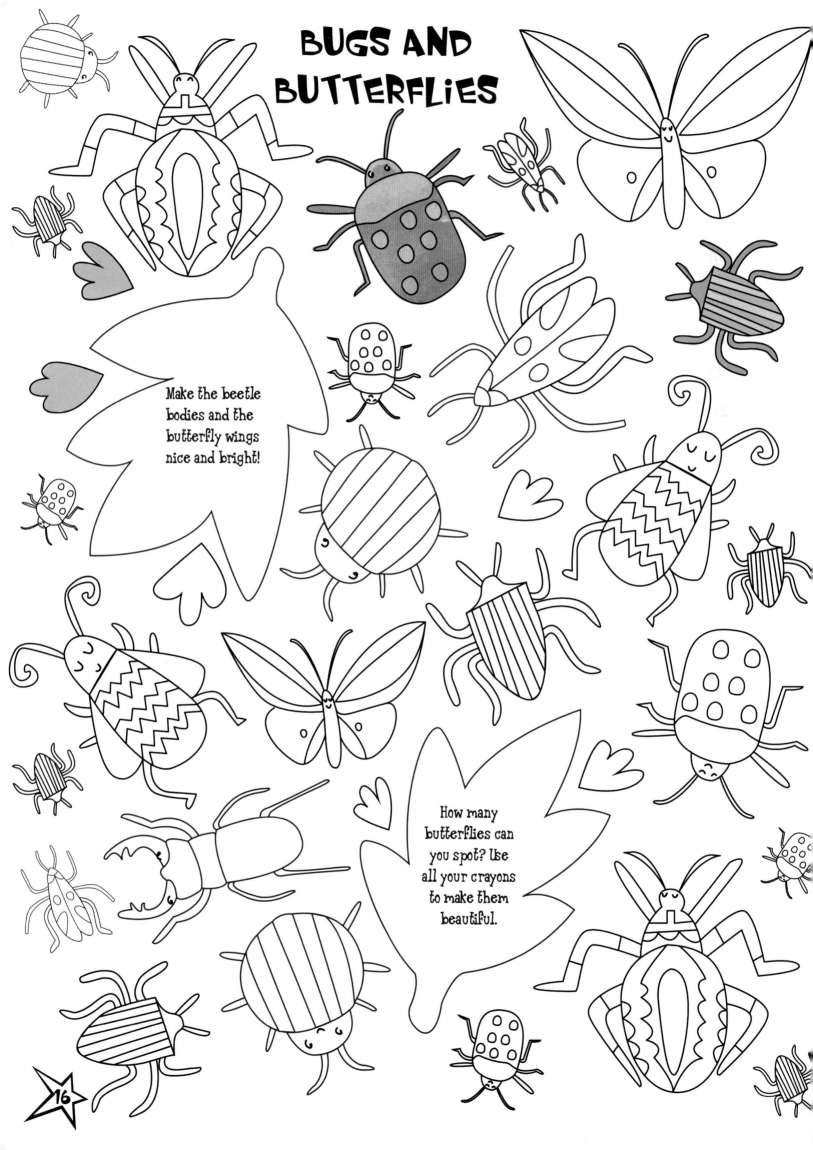

BUGS AND BUTTERFLIES

Make the beetle bodies and the butterfly wings nice and bright!

How many butterflies can you spot? Use all your crayons to make them beautiful.

16

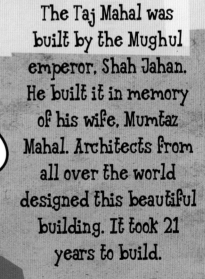

This is a
5 RUPEE coin.

iNDiA

We're going to Ranthambore National Park in India. Help us search for tigers sneaking, snoozing and splashing with their cubs!

Namaste

The Taj Mahal was built by the Mughul emperor, Shah Jahan. He built it in memory of his wife, Mumtaz Mahal. Architects from all over the world designed this beautiful building. It took 21 years to build.

Fill the truck with your stickers. Don't forget your insect repellent, camera and walking boots.

Have fun sticking on the animal families who live in the Indian Jungle.

Find a bright green chameleon and pop on a friend for him to play with.

Tigers are the biggest cats in the world. This one is 6 feet (2 metres) long.

I turn bright green when I'm very happy!

18

People keep their eyes peeled in the **RANTHAMBORE** National Park for a glimpse of a roaming tiger or a shy sloth bear.

Can you spot the big wide eyes of a loris?

Baloo from Rudyard Kipling's *Jungle Book* was a sloth bear just like this one. Add some fruit for him to snack on.

Gibbons are the noisiest apes!

SPLASHING ELEPHANTS

Get out your pencils and make the elephants look bright and beautiful.

How many baby elephants can you count?
Paint the splashing water blue.

Olà

Let's sail to the Galápagos Islands, Ecuador! We'll meet ancient tortoises, huge iguanas, funny birds and friendly sea lions.

THE GALÁPAGOS

Fill the pelican's beak with creatures from the sea.

The Galápagos Islands were discovered by the Spanish in 1535. The name 'galápago' means 'tortoise' in Spanish.

This is a DOLLAR note.

Find your stickers and fill the islands with busy creatures.

Can you spot a blue footed booby? Give him some blue footed friends.

Sea Lions are slow on land but can travel as fast as a car in water (up to 25 miles or 40 km per hour). Pop a slow sea lion on land.

The wild and wonderful creatures of **THE GALÁPAGOS** are fearless. They'll let you get close. Here you'll find some of the world's rarest animals.

Atishoo!

Marina Iguanas sneeze to clear sea salt out of their noses and it often lands on their head! Add some more sneezing iguanas and say bless you!

GIANT TORTOISE

Watch them feed on the prickly cactus.

Use your crayons to brighten up the tortoise shells.

Give the prickly cactus red flowers.

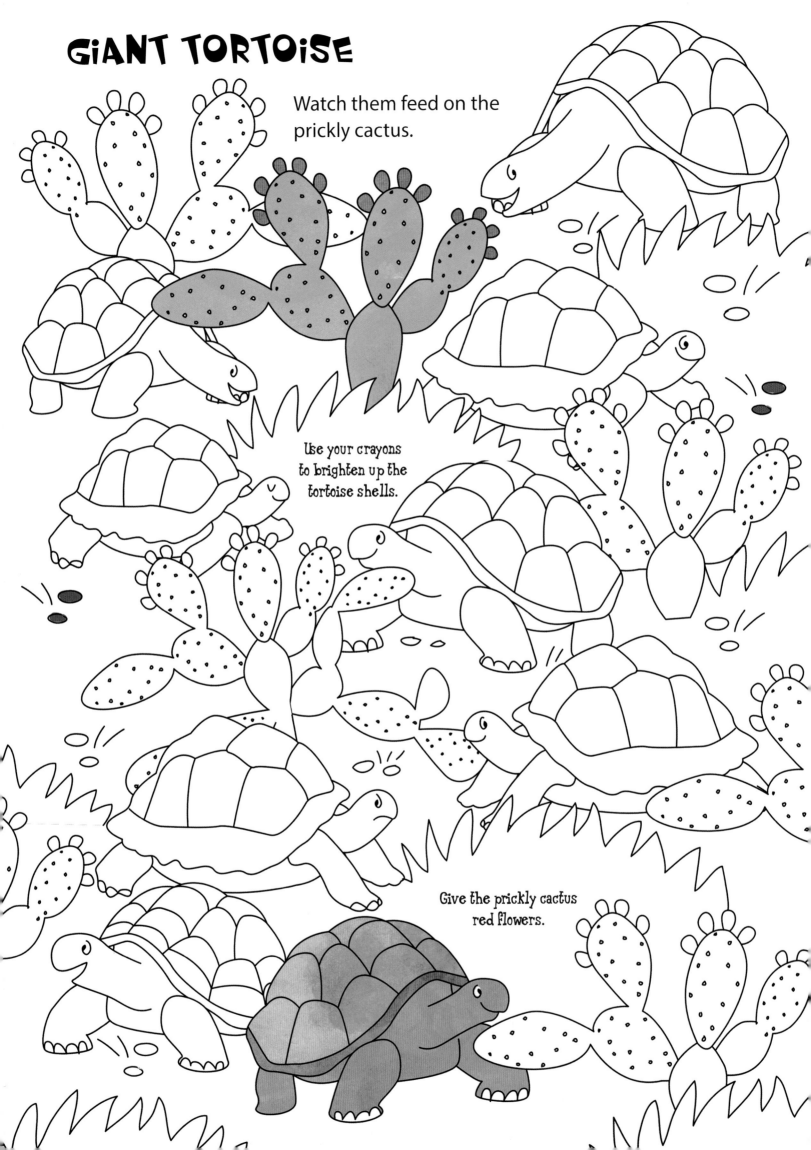

Nihao

CHiNA

Travel to Huanglong in China with us! We can't wait to meet giant black and white pandas, small red pandas and cuddly monkeys with blue faces!

In China there's not only the Great Wall of China, the longest ever built, but also the world's only giant pandas. You'll find them near the Yangtze River.

We'll probably get hungry later. Let's pack some Chinese food and drink to take into the mountains with us.

This is a 20 Yuan note.

Find your stickers and fill the forest with magical animals.

Look for a Sichuan takin and give him some friends. He has horns on his head and special thick oily fur that keeps the water off him when it rains.

Giant pandas love to eat bamboo, which is a woody type of grass. Give some bamboo to the pandas.

Hi

Fly with us to Florida, USA. We're going to wade into the Everglades to get as close as we dare to alligators. Then we'll meet some smelly skunks!

USA

Did you know, when alligators are young they have yellow stripes on their tail? As they get older, these stripes get darker.

Help us to pack for our trip to the Everglades. We'll need sunglasses, a camera and binoculars.

This is a DOLLAR note.

Bald headed eagles like to stay with one eagle for life. Give this bald eagle a special eagle friend.

Can you see the mummy alligator with her eggs?

Snap your alligator stickers onto the page. Then find out what other creatures live here.

People call this area of **THE EVERGLADES** Ten Thousand Islands. There are lots of islands and lots of alligators to SNAP a photo of.

Give the pelican a couple of friends.

Look for a shy manatee poking her nose out of the water.

FLASHY FLAMINGOS

Decorate these beautifully elegant birds.

How many hummingbirds can you spot?

Find the flamingos and make them bright pink.

Give the pelicans brightly painted beaks.

Hallo

GERMANY

When we go to the Bavarian Forest today, we're sure of a big surprise! Big brown bears, wild cats, teeny tiny owls and hairy pigs live in this German forest.

The Brothers Grimm wrote famous children's fairy tales set in Bavaria, including Cinderella, Rapunzel, Red Riding Hood and Snow White.

This is a EURO!

Pack the bicycle basket for your trip to the Bavarian Forest. Take food, a drink and something in case it rains.

Pop on lots of bears having fun, and find out what other wild animals live in the German forest.

Bears carry their cubs, splish splash in lakes and slide in the snow with their friends in the **BAVARIAN FOREST.**

TREE-TOP FUN

Look who's hiding in the woods.

Make the bears brown and paint the leaves green.

Can you spot the two sleepy owls? Make them orange.

Hello

PACIFIC OCEAN

Follow the Deepsea Challenger sub into the deepest darkest ocean on Earth and discover some really weird alien creatures.

The Marinana Trench is one of the world's oldest and deepest seabeds. It is more than 7 miles (20 kilometres) deep and over 180 million years old.

Hide your sea creatures stickers amongst the coral.

Find your stickers
and fill the ocean
with amazing
creatures.

The film director,
James Cameron, dived
to the bottom of Mariana
Trench in a sub he
designed himself. It's
called the DEEPSEA
CHALLENGER.

Anglerfish
have glow in the dark
tentacles to attract other
fish, which they then
gobble up. Add another
Anglerfish, but be
careful he doesn't nibble
your fingers.

MARIANA TRENCH

These black waters are freezing and very very deep. It takes a special kind of creature to survive living here.

Hydrothermal vents are hot and bubbly so some animals like to live around them.

AUSTRALIA

Uluru is sometimes known as Ayers Rock. It's a large sandstone rock. If you're feeling energetic you can climb to the top!

Let's visit Uluru, in the desert Outback of Australia. Look out for hopping kangaroos, galloping emu and koalas hanging in the trees.

G'day!

This is a dollar coin.

Give the kangaroo a hat. Use her pouch to store a boomerang to throw and a didgeridoo to play some music.

Hop some stickers onto this page and have fun filling the land with unusual animals.

Koalas are often called bears because they look a little like teddy bears, but they are actually marsupials. The mother koala uses her pouch to carry her baby, called a joey.

A big green emu egg is only a little bit smaller than your head! Add a few more eggs to the pile. Quick, before they hatch!

People come to see the sun rise over this huge beautiful rock called Uluru in the **OUTBACK** of Australia. It's also a great place to spot Australia's weird and wonderful creatures in the wild.

Wave at the flying doctor in the plane! The Outback is so far away from cities that doctors fly to help people who are sick or injured.

Kangaroos carry their children in a pouch on their tummy. Add another kangaroo and her baby here.

The frilled lizard of Australia is sometimes called the 'bicycle' lizard. This is because it runs on its hind legs when it is scared.

PRETTY PARROTS

Get your crayons out and make the birds bold and bright.

Paint the parrots green, red and yellow.

Can you spot kookaburras? Paint thier beaks yellow.

How many butterflies do you see? Make them really bright.

44

DIVING DIFFERENCES

Spot 6 differences between these two pictures.

Answers on page 48

45

WILD SHADOWS

Can you match the animals with their shadows?
Draw a line with your crayons from the animal to its shadow.

Answers on page 48

MOVING MAZE

Pick your ride and see where the road will take you.

Answers on page 48

ANSWERS FOR PAGES 45, 46 AND 47

DIVING DIFFERENCES

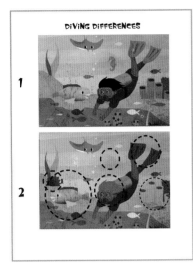

1

2

WILD SHADOWS

MOVING MAZE

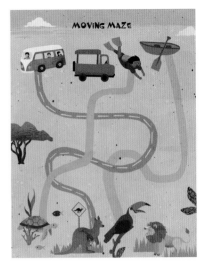

1. The diver's flippers change to red in 2.
2. The diver's hair changes to yellow in 2.
3. The seahorse disappears in 2.
4. The green fish swims in the opposite direction in 2.
5. The coral on the right changes to blue in 2.
6. The red coral on the left appears in 2.

1. The campervan takes you to the kangaroo.
2. The truck takes you to the lion.
3. The diver takes you to the turtle.
4. The boat takes you to the toucan.

Published in October 2014 by Lonely Planet Global Limited
ABN 36 005 607 983
www.lonelyplanet.com
ISBN 978 1 74360 396 3
© Lonely Planet 2014
© Photographs as indicated 2014
Printed in China   10 9 8 7 6 5

Publishing Director	Piers Pickard
Publisher	Mina Patria
Art Director & Designer	Beverley Speight
Author	Sara Oldham
Illustrator	Frann Preston-Gannon
	Pippa Curnick - black and white colouring pages
Pre-press production	Tag Response
Print production	Larissa Frost
Thanks to	Jessica Cole

Lonely Planet offices

AUSTRALIA
The Malt Store, Level 3, 551 Swanston St, Carlton, Victoria 3053. T: 03 8379 8000

IRELAND
Digital Depot, Roe Lane (off Thomas St), Digital Hub, Dublin 8, D08 TCV4

USA
124 Linden St, Oakland, CA 94607. T: 510 250 6400

UNITED KINGDOM
240 Blackfriars Rd, London SE1 8NW. T: 020 3771 5100

STAY IN TOUCH lonelyplanet.com/contact

p. 2-3

p. 4

USA p.29

Germany p. 33

China p. 25

India p.17

Africa p.5

Australia p.41

Galapagos p. 21

Pacific Ocean p. 37

3D model

Brazil p. 13

Egypt p. 9

Pacific Ocean

Kruger p . 6-7

Red Sea p. 10-11

Amazon p. 14-15

Ranthambore p. 18-19

avaria p.34-35

Mariana Trench
p. 38—39

Outback p. 42-43